KEEP COOL!

Strategies for managing anger at school

••••••••••••

Paula Galey

Pembroke Publishers Limited

© 2004 User Friendly Resource Enterprises Ltd.

Pembroke Publishers

538 Hood Road
Markham, Ontario, Canada L3R 3K9
www.pembrokepublishers.com

Distributed in the U.S. by Stenhouse Publishers
477 Congress Street
Portland, ME 04101
www.stenhouse.com

This edition is adapted from *Keep Cool* originally published by User friendly Resource Enterprises Ltd. in New Zealand in 2003.

Thanks to Kathy Paterson for her contribution to this edition.

National Library of Canada Cataloguing in Publication

Galey, Paula
        Keep cool!: strategies for managing anger at school / Paula Galey.

ISBN 1-55138-168-0

        1. Anger in children.   2. Bullying in schools—Prevention.
3. Aggressiveness in children.   4. School violence—Prevention. I. Title.

BF723.A4G34 2004   372.17'82   C2003-907106-5

Editor: Pauline Scanlan, Carol-Ann Freeman
Cover Design: John Zehethofer
Cover Photo: Ajay Photographics
Layout Design: Jay Tee Graphics Ltd.
Design & Illustrations: Akira LeFevre

Printed and bound in Canada
9 8 7 6 5 4 3 2 1

Contents

Foreword

It happened in the blink of an eye. The boy shot up angrily, sent his desk flying, and stormed out the door, slamming it loudly behind him. There was a moment of agonizing silence while the other students watched me with wide eyes, wondering what I was going to do. With a hasty, "keep working," I dashed after the boy. A series of questions bombarded my brain, *Where did he go? What should I do? Why was he so upset? What would the principal say? What about his parents?* I didn't have long to query. He was at the exit to the school where he was repeatedly hurling himself at the door clearly marked "pull". I watched in horror as the window shook and the door shuddered each time his tiny body was used as a battering ram over and over again. Driven by adrenaline I charged forward and grabbed him from behind, attempting to trap the flying arms in a hug of sorts. My only thought was to stop him from hurting himself. Within seconds we were on the floor, rolling together in an absurd melee of arms and legs. *How could a ten year old be so strong?* After what seemed like hours, his body went limp, all explosive anger spent, and it was over — this time!

At the back of the room the girl sat with sullen, downcast eyes, staring intently at the pencil with the jagged, broken tip. She had been using it to scratch deep, nasty looking gouges into her forearm. Here and there beads of blood had broken the surface and she rubbed at them aimlessly, spreading the bright red across her arm. I stood before her, shocked, silent! Even as I watched in horror, she dug the pencil into her flesh once more. Not knowing what else to do I held out my hand. She sighed quietly and gave me the offending weapon, for she was not abusive — to anyone other than herself — and neither was she "out of control" or in the throes of a tantrum. Her anger was turned inward.

Although the manifestations of anger displayed by both of these children may seem extreme, they are not unusual in many classrooms. In both cases, the children were angry — furious, in fact, but each dealt with the emotion very differently. Other children, all children if truth be told, experience anger too, and must find within themselves ways to cope with their discomfort. For many of them, that anger is a terrible monster that can rob them of happiness and cause unnecessary problems both at home and at school because they do not have the necessary resources, knowledge and wisdom to deal effectively with their anger.

As adults we know that anger is normal, even useful. It is a natural emotion that allows us to grow and to develop new techniques, strategies, relationships and self-awareness. We know, also, that anger *unchecked* can result in a vast number of negative consequences just as anger *unleashed* can have equally disastrous ramifications. So we learn to channel our anger — to avoid turning it inward while at the same time not allowing it to erupt into displays of bad temper (most of the time). Children, however, are not so fortunate. They don't have years of practice in anger management. And for many of them, anger is an uncontrollable force that makes their lives miserable. They are lacking the tools to deal with this inner turmoil; they don't know when, or how, to say to themselves, "Stop!"

Children's anger can be likened to the physical discomfort of a developing blister. Consider walking in a new pair of shoes. A slight rubbing is noticed at the heel. It begins innocently — a tiny annoyance that, although uncomfortable, can be quite easily overlooked. *Compare this to the irritation a child feels at some aspect of his or her life over which he or she has little or no control.* As the blister grows and its presence becomes more painful, most adults, given that the shoes are new, will elect to ignore the discomfort and keep going. A rational choice has been made after taking into account the pros and cons of the situation as well as the consequences of either action or inaction. *The anger in the child, however, grows steadily too, and, not having the knowledge of pros, cons, choices and consequences, also "keeps going".* Eventually the blister breaks the skin, decorating the sock with an unappealing bloody smudge, and the spikes of pain cause the adult to take immediate action, all the while berating him or herself for not doing so sooner. *The child's pain spikes too, and she or he reacts, often in an inappropriate manner. Due to lack of experience, his or her choices were limited largely to "striking out," at self or others.*

As concerned adults, then, it is our responsibility to help children in our care to understand anger, to be able to recognize it in its early stages and find suitable ways of managing it — to know when to "take the shoe off". Like other childhood life skills, these skills can be taught, practiced, encouraged and learned.

We know that what is not understood is frightening. If children do not understand their anger, or how to handle it, the accompanying fear can be paralyzing. Since we cannot necessarily remove the cause(s) of their anger, let's teach them awareness and reaction tactics. Let's give them the tools to overcome this potential fear and to use their natural anger in a positive manner. Let's show them they have the power to deal effectively with their anger. Let's teach them to "Keep Cool".

This book shares numerous practical suggestions for anger management in children. (It comes to mind that a lot of adults might pay heed to the ideas as well.) Teachers want their students to be successful, not just at school but at *life*. Given that anger will be a part of their "forever lives," what better way to help them achieve success than by consciously coaching them in many different ways to contend with anger rather than leave it unmanaged?

The following excerpt from Henry Wadsworth Longfellow's *The Courtship of Miles Standish* beautifully captures the notion of the dangers of unmanaged anger.

> "There are moments in life when the heart is so full of emotion
> That if by chance it be shaken, or into its depths like a pebble
> Drops some careless word, it overflows, and its secret,
> Spilt on the ground like water, can never be gathered together."

By using the ideas offered in *Keep Cool*, teachers will be able to help their students deal with hearts full of angry emotion so that they can react appropriately *before* that final pebble causes irreparable scattering and pain.

In *Keep Cool*, numerous strategies, teaching suggestions and hands-on activities for children will empower teachers to show children ways to manage their anger. Use the book as a tool to help you become a better teacher and your students to become better "anger managers". This is a learning situation where everyone wins!

Good luck — and remember — *keep your cool* as well!

Kathy Paterson

Introduction

Keep Cool! has been developed to assist teachers and others who are working with those students who respond to conflict or challenges with inappropriate actions or with aggressive behaviour.

The resource provides teachers with guidance and frameworks that focus on skills and strategies that will allow students to respond to challenging situations in ways which are acceptable to others. Students will learn to understand what triggers their anger and also to understand that they can make choices about how to respond when they feel angry.

The strategies students learn will help them to pay attention to the physiological and psychological processes they undergo at the point of becoming angry and sets out practical skills they can implement to calm themselves down. Additionally, students will develop an understanding of the difference between 'good' anger and 'bad' anger.

When students are able to respond to their feelings of anger with a wide range of strategies they will feel a sense of personal power and be able to exercise greater self-control.

Using this Resource

The material in this resource can be used:
- with all students as part of the health curriculum
- by specialist staff such as guidance counsellors, behaviour support workers on an individual basis with at-risk students
- in peer tutoring schemes using senior students in life skills classes with at-risk junior students
- with small groups of at-risk students working with a teacher's assistant
- by parents or caregivers working with their children individually in the home.

Resource Structure

The resource is divided into six sections. Each has been developed to take about one hour to complete. It is a good idea if users aim to work through the sections in order as the process is structured developmentally. However teachers should also feel free to use the material more flexibly to align it with the learning needs of their students.

Each section begins with teacher guidelines, supported by student activity sheets. Sessions should ideally begin with a rapport building activity followed by a review of previous learning.

There are several activities included in the introduction that were developed to help students monitor and deal effectively with their anger. The activities are ***Awareness Window*** (p. 17), ***Mood Graph*** (p. 19), ***Knocking Down Walls*** (p.20) and ***Balloon Float*** (p. 22). There will be opportunities to use these activities throughout the book or you may wish to use these activities to introduce students to the topic of anger management.

Most teachers find themselves needing to deal with the issue of anger in the classroom at some time or other. This initial section summarizes some current thinking about what anger is, how it can manifest itself – both positively and negatively – and what it means for the students you work with.

What is anger?

Anger is an emotion, not a behavior. It's a particular kind of response to an external trigger. Like all responses, we're all triggered by different things.

Common anger triggers can be:

- feeling hurt
- feeling betrayed
- feeling frustrated
- feeling insecure
- feeling afraid
- feeling wronged
- feeling a sense of injustice
- feeling powerless
- feeling embarrassed
- feeling jealous.

Similarly the depth and range of the anger felt will manifest itself as different behaviors in different people. Some people become silent, others become enraged enough to hit out. There is almost always a physical manifestation of anger, even if it is stored away (sometimes for years).

Anger is not a bad thing. It is a physiologically important emotion which can motivate us into action. For example, if we see someone mistreating an animal, our anger will motivate us into trying to stop the mistreatment. Many great social movements have been generated through mass anger against perceived injustices.

Problems with anger almost always arise when people use the feelings of drive and energy which are triggered in ways that cause negative consequences. This is where anger management comes into play. Managing anger means consciously recognizing that you are angry and then deciding how you will deal with the energy. Good anger management involves using the energy to fuel some type of action that will resolve the problem or diffuse the emotion without violating the rights of others.

When we are angry our repertoire of responses can be defined by many things including:

- how old we are
- how we've seen others deal with anger as we grew up
- the threshold of our endurance
- whether we've been shown ways that we can deal with anger
- whether we are under the influence of alcohol or drugs
- how we've dealt with anger in the past and whether it worked.

Anger at School

A healthy school environment is one where students feel safe. Their sense of safety will come from many things:

- knowing how members of the school community are expected to behave towards each other
- knowing what the boundaries of individual behaviour are
- knowing that all people in the school community are cared for and respected
- knowing that there is zero tolerance for bullying, hitting out and put-downs
- knowing that the school has a range of frameworks in place that allow people to deal with their anger, including: time out, counselling, conflict resolution, or other interventions.

If you look back at the anger triggers you'll see that schools must be minefields in terms of potential for angry feelings! Although the incidents that trigger anger are likely to be different for a six-year-old ("I don't want to do the cross country!") and a sixteen-year-old ("I deserved an A for that essay!"). The feeling beneath the anger will be the same – "I feel threatened or powerless". We might expect sixteen-year-olds to have better ways of dealing with their feelings than six-year-olds, but this will only happen for many if they have *learned* strategies for dealing with it.

Teacher Modelling

If you get angry in class (and most of us do) and manifest your anger in negative ways like shouting uncontrollably at individuals, storming around and so on, it will be pretty difficult to deliver an anger management programme with credibility. So look at yourself first and how you deal with conflict and crisis. How you manage these things yourself will provide the most significant example to your students of alternative ways of expressing your frustration or displeasure at a situation. Showing that you can keep cool under pressure demonstrates what self-control is all about. You'll send the message, "It may look like a crisis, but by staying cool I'll be in a better position to solve the problem." Use "I" messages to show your annoyance. They'll soon get the message.

This is particularly important for students who have not seen this kind of approach to dealing with feelings of anger modelled at home. Research shows that family background can play a role in how easily children are angered. Typically, angry children come from families that are disruptive, chaotic and not skilled at emotional communication. It's important too when our children are bombarded with media images of angry people solving problems by shooting each other.

About The Hassle Log

The Hassle Log is an important part of this resource. It has been designed to help students learn the skills of assessing their own behavior and monitoring their own progress over how they manage their anger. It presents a structured 'non-judgemental' framework for students to reflect on how they handled their anger in a given situation. The log should be used at every session where anger is the focus.

Many students will also benefit from keeping a journal in which they paste their Hassle Log over a negotiated period of time, perhaps a week or two weeks.

The Hassle Log should be seen as a platform for learning. If students record negative experiences about their anger – this is an opportunity to address what happened and to plan for a different outcome next time.

Starting off each session

- Begin each session on anger in the same way. Ask students to think about the most recent thing that happened to make them feel angry.
- Individuals can spend a quiet few minutes completing the Hassle Log about this incident.
- Those who want to tell the group their most recent 'angry' stories can do so. Use this opportunity to focus on what they did, how they think they handled the situation and what they could have done differently. Focus too on drawing out what the consequences of their actions were / might be.
- For students to feel confident telling their stories, aim for this to be an open forum where judgements aren't made. Use questions like:

  - What did you do then?
  - How did you feel?
  - Why do you think you felt like that?
  - How might the other person have felt?
  - What could you have done differently?

Emphasize the need for confidentiality, "What's said within this room stays within this room."

Discussions can be led by the teacher at first, modelling questions, later other students can take on this facilitating role. Build up confidence in students role-playing other people's 'angry' stories and see if they are able to come up with alternative outcomes for each other.

THE HASSLE LOG

NAME _____ DATE _____

This is what happened

Someone teased me ☐   Someone took my things ☐

Someone ordered me about ☐   Someone started a fight with me ☐

Someone did something I didn't like ☐   I did something wrong ☐

Other_____

This is when it happened

In Class ☐   After school ☐   Before school ☐

Recess ☐   Lunch time ☐   At home ☐

Other_____

This is how angry I felt

Annoyed ☐   Quite angry ☐   Angry ☐   Really Angry ☐   Burning ☐

This is who made me angry

Student ☐   Teacher ☐   Staff member ☐

Parent ☐   Family ☐   Someone else _____

This is what I did

Hit back	☐	Kicked	☐	Yelled	☐
Swore	☐	Argued	☐	Cried	☐
Ran away	☐	Went silent	☐	Hurt myself	☐
Hid somewhere	☐	Got revenge	☐	Negotiated	☐
Compromised	☐	Took time out	☐	Talked about it	☐
Asserted myself	☐	Ignored it	☐	Damaged property	☐
Told someone	☐	Calmed down	☐	Thought of the consequences	☐
Got help	☐	Other _____			

This is how I handled the situation

Very well ☐   OK ☐   Not well at all ☐

The outcome of the situation was…

This is what I would do differently next time

The Anger Control Game
(AKA The Sweet Game)

Information for Teachers

This is a good starter activity. But be warned… students will get angry! The game students will play here is designed to be unfair. Its purpose to get people talking about anger and how they felt during the game. The situation is controlled but make sure that you read through the rules carefully before you begin playing the game. Try playing it with some colleagues first so that you get the idea.

Number of Players

3 – 15

Resources

A copy of the rules for each person
Two identical packs of cards
Pair of dice
Bowl
Bag of individually wrapped sweets – enough for 5 each

GETTING STARTED

Before you start, secretly remove two hearts from one of the packs of cards. Replace the hearts with two cards of a different suit from the spare pack so that you still have 52. Make sure that you mix the remaining hearts so that they are more towards the top of the pack. Decide how long you want the game to be; this might be a time limit, or when a certain number of players have been eliminated, or when the bowl has a certain number of sweets in it. At the end of the game you will select the person who has shown the best sportspersonship (you), and you will take all the sweets out of the bowl for yourself.

Don't tell them that this is called the Anger Control Game! At least not until you've explained what you've been doing. Call it the Sweet Game!

FOLLOW-UP

After you've played this infuriating game, you will have a group of annoyed students who will complain about the game's unfairness. Use this focus and energy to discuss these questions. Make sure you set up this part so that people are not calling out.

1. Did you enjoy this game? Why or why not?
2. How are you feeling right now, especially physically?
3. What do you think is causing you to feel like this?
4. What other kinds of things can make you feel this way?
5. What different sorts of actions can you take when you are faced with situations that make you feel angry?

The Sweet Game

How to Play

1. Players sit in a circle and each person has 5 sweets. You are not allowed to eat the sweets.
2. Put the bowl in the middle of the table.
3. Everyone must have a copy of the rules next to them.
4. Decide who will start the game.
5. When it's your turn you can choose between rolling the dice or choosing a card.

Dice

If you choose to roll the dice – add the two numbers together.
If the number is:
ODD – put a sweet in the bowl.
EVEN – take a sweet from anyone else's pile
If a **DOUBLE** is thrown (you don't add these together) give anyone playing one of your sweets.

Cards

If you choose to draw a card and you get a:
SPADE – you must give a sweet to the person on your right.
CLUB – you must give a sweet to the person on your left.
DIAMOND – you must put a sweet in the bowl.
HEART – you get two sweets from the bowl (or from a person of your choice if the bowl is empty.)

6. If you lose all your sweets you are out of the game.
7. You can get back in the game if someone gives you a sweet after one of their turns.
8. At the end of the game the person with the most sweets wins, and everyone else may keep any sweets they have won.
9. Your teacher will decide who displayed the best sportsmanship during the game – and this person gets any remaining sweets from the bowl.

Awareness Window

Information for Teachers

This is a good activity to help students learn more about themselves; the more they know, the better able they will be to understand what angers them, and what the early warning signs of their anger might be. Use this activity at various times of the year to allow students to compare their current windows to the ones they made previously. Has anything changed? If so, why? Is there anything they can do about the change?

Resources

Awareness Window (p. 17), enough copies for each student in class

GETTING STARTED

- Before you hand out the Awareness Window to students, draw a vertical and horizontal line intersecting each other on the board, resembling the four quarters of a window. In each quadrant write each of the following headings: public self, unknown self, angry self and private self.
- With the help of the students, write down words under the heading public self that describe you as others know you (e.g., tall, helpful, happy). In the unknown self, list things that you don't know about yourself at this particular moment (e.g. "Will my cold get better?", "When will I complete my marking?"). In the angry self, write words that indicate things that may be annoying you at this particular time (e.g., "lost pen," "too much talking"). Do not fill in the quadrant labelled private self explaining that this quadrant is only meant for you to know about, unless you choose to share it with others.
- Hand out copies of **Awareness Window** (p. 17) for students to complete. You may wish to organize students into small groups to work together. Remind students that the private self doesn't need to be filled in, but encourage students to think of what they would like to put there.

FOLLOW-UP

Older students can choose one word or phrase from each quadrant to write about, or, choose all the items from one quadrant to write about. Younger students can do a similar activity with illustrations.

As a class, discuss the following questions:
- Did you learn anything new about yourself? What did you learn?
- Which "window" did you write the most in? Why?
- What can you do about the items written in the angry window?
- Which window has changed the most from the last time you did this activity?
- Is it possible that some of these windows will stay the same?
- Do any of the items in the private self make you angry or upset?
- Are there items in the private self that you want to share?

AWARENESS WINDOW

This activity will help you learn more about yourself. Complete each of the following boxes:

Public self: Describe yourself as others know you (e.g., tall, shy, happy).

Unknown self: Describe things about yourself that you don't know at this particular moment (e.g. "Will I get a good mark on my math text?", "When will my cold get better?")

Angry self: Write down things that are annoying you at this particular time (e.g., "My bus being late for school.", "My friend is not listening to me.")

Private self: You don't have to write answers in this section, but try to think of what you might like to include.

Public self	Unknown self
Angry self	**Private self**

Mood Graph

Information for Teachers

Similar to the **Awareness Window**, this activity gives students an opportunity to examine how they are feeling and to relate these feelings to specific times or activities. Knowing themselves better will be a student's first step in learning to deal with emotions, including anger.

Resources

Mood Graph (p. 19), enough copies for each student in class

GETTING STARTED

- Draw a horizontal line on the board.
- Divide the line into three or four sections by placing dark dots at regular intervals.
- Draw a small happy face above the line and small sad face under the line. (see **Mood Graph**, p. 19)
- Tell students that you are feeling excited because they are about to start something new. Then draw an arrow starting at the first dot pointing upward. At the tip of the arrow, write the reason for your happiness in one or two words. Explain to students that the higher or lower the arrow goes from the baseline, the stronger the emotion is.
- Explain that you and the class will do this 4 times during the day to see how feelings change over the course of the day. (It is a good idea to select times when you feel students are really happy, really upset, or tired so that emotions are obvious.)
- Hand out a copy of **Mood Graph** (p. 19) to each student.
- Younger students can draw happy, sad, excited or angry faces as opposed to writing words.

FOLLOW-UP

- At the end of the day, examine the graphs and discuss the "highs and lows".
- Encourage students to make their own mood graphs to evaluate their feelings at any time of the day they choose.

MOOD GRAPH

You can use this graph to monitor your feelings to show when you are happy, sad, angry, or just doing fine. Draw a vertical line (the longer the line, the stronger the emotion) to indicate how you are feeling. At the top of the line, using one or two words, write why you are feeling that way.

Knocking Down Walls

Information for Teachers

This activity is a long-term classroom activity that allows students an opportunity to identify and express their feelings of anger in a positive way and also gives students an opportunity to help another student deal with their anger. Although this activity has metaphorical implications that younger children may not understand, they will benefit from the exercise nonetheless.

Each student is given a small personal section of a wall in the classroom. The area doesn't have to be big; about two feet square is sufficient, but it must be clearly marked with the student's name. You may wish to use a section of wall at the back of the room, divided into "Personal Spaces" using masking tape as lines. These personal spaces can be used for a variety of things: students may wish to post notes or birthday greetings to each other or they may wish to display their work. For this activity, students will be using their personal spaces to post "Bad Feeling Bricks". Bad Feeling Bricks (BFBs) are rectangles, about the size of a common brick, cut from red construction paper. At any time during the day when a student is feeling upset or sensing the beginnings of anger, he can take a brick, write on it what emotion he is feeling, what is upsetting him, or even leave it blank. The brick is then attached to his personal space for all to see. If other bricks are added, they are placed to form a wall.

```
          ┌─────────────┐
          │  Feel mad   │
      ┌───────────┬───────────┐
      │ Can't do  │ my pencil │
      │ this work │  broke    │
      └───────────┴───────────┘
          │  Samantha   │
          │   hit me    │
          └─────────────┘
```

The object of the activity is two-fold.

1. The student is able to identify a negative situation and express how they feel.
2. Others can readily see what's happening and can try to help.

In other words, if another child can do something to "remove a brick," the teacher encourages him to do so. For example, Samantha could apologize, and remove that particular brick, thereby "knocking down the wall" somewhat. Another child may offer to help this child with his work.

If a student places a brick on her personal space, but there is no writing on it, you can quietly ask the child what is going on and hopefully an intervention can be made before anger erupts. I once watched a grade three boy add as many unmarked bricks as he could fit into his square. He quickly filled his personal space to become a solid brick wall. I quietly sat down beside him and asked him if he wanted to talk at recess. He nodded glumly. At recess a torrent of tears quickly indicated the inner turmoil this student was feeling, and we were able to deal with his problem appropriately. Had it not been for the "wall" I may not have known so quickly that something was wrong.

GETTING STARTED

- As a class, discuss the walls that make up buildings and homes and the reasons we need them (e.g., protection, privacy). Then discuss the imaginary walls that people sometimes build around themselves for security, privacy and protection. Ask students: Why may people want to build imaginary walls around themselves?
- Discuss ways to break down these walls (e.g., invite someone to join a team or group, write a positive note to someone, offer to help someone, apologize if necessary).
- Together, make a collage showing ways that students can "break down walls". The display could include drawings, magazine pictures, writings or words. Create a title for the collage and display it in a prominent place in the class.
- Discuss what a personal space is by modeling your own personal space and adding a couple of bricks to it. Then give students time to think of ways they can help you remove the bricks to "knock down your wall". Emphasize the importance to ensure that a student's wall doesn't get too big and encourage students to take part in trying to knock down walls as they arise.

Note: At first the students may be reluctant to put bricks up or to take steps to knock another student's bricks down. Or, conversely, students may want to fill their entire personal spaces with bricks. Be patient and reinforce the rules. Soon students will use the idea carefully and conscientiously.

FOLLOW-UP

- Students can write reflections about their use, or lack of use, of their personal space.
- Partners can work together to offer advice about each other's walls.
- Students can write letters to parents explaining one positive thing that happened as a result of their wall.

Balloon Float

Information for Teachers

The simple act of hitting balloons (2 – 4 at a time) as hard as possible helps to release anger and vent emotions. In addition, this is a cooperative game that is fun for everyone. Break the class into teams of four to six players and have each group stand or sit in a small circle. Sitting on the floor makes the game more difficult, especially if "not standing up" becomes one of the rules. Explain the rules of the game and be sure students know there is to be no "hitting directly *at* people".

Number of Players

Teams of 4–6

Resources

2–4 balloons per team

Note: Do not blow up the ballons to full capacity – they will be more likely to break.

GETTING STARTED

- Divide class into teams of 4–6 students.
- Blow up balloons and give each team 2–4 differently colored balloons.
- The object of this game is to keep the balloons in the air as long as possible while everyone on the team must hit each color of balloon at least once. (You can hit a balloon as often as necessary to keep it afloat.) Remind students that this is a team effort so all players must work together.
- Students can hit the balloons as hard as they want but if a balloon breaks, their team loses.
- After everyone in the group has hit each color, (encourage honesty about this) then the quest is to see how long all of the balloons can be kept afloat.
- If the balloon hits the floor, leave it there.
- The team that keeps the most balloons in the air the longest wins.

FOLLOW-UP

After playing this game, discuss these questions with students:

- What did it feel like to be part of a group that worked together?
- Did you like hitting the balloons? Why?
- Who hit the balloons the hardest in your group?
- How did you cooperate to help everyone hit each color?
- Did anyone feel angry during the game? Why or why not?
- How could you use an activity like this if you were feeling angry at home?

1. Where Does My Anger Come From?

Key Ideas

What's good about anger? What's bad about anger? Can we change our behaviors? Why does how we behave matter?

Starting Off Ideas

- Talk about the idea of good and bad anger. Is it ever good to be angry? When is it bad?
- Play the **Anger Control Game** (p. 14) and discuss students' feelings of anger.
- Tell stories about being angry. What was the angriest you've ever been? What made you angry? What did you do?
- What kinds of things make you angry?
- Draw anger. What does it look like? How big is it? What color is it?
- Write this sentence starter: "I feel angry when…" Tell students that they can write as many sentences as they like that begin with these words. They might like to do this on big sheets of paper in pairs – using different colored pens.

(Habits) Let's Talk About Habits

- Use the Portia Nelson poem ***Autobiography in Five Short Chapters*** (p. 25) with students. It illustrates how people can fall into the same pattern of behavior even though they know the end result will be bad. Talk about habits that they have. What good habits do people have? (brushing teeth) What bad habits do they have? (biting nails) Where do habits come from? How are habits broken? Do they have any *behaviors* that are 'habits'? (like sulking if they lose a game).

- Talk about how breaking a habit, especially if it's a bad one, takes:
  Self-awareness (of the habit)
  Conscience (knowing what's good /bad, right / wrong, how it affects others)
  Imagination (seeing alternatives and choices)
  Will power (consciously deciding to change, actually changing and sticking to the change)
  Ask someone to volunteer a 'bad habit' that they think they have. See if students can discuss how to apply these qualities to help the person to change the habit. Move onto the activity sheet ***Can You Break the Habit?*** (p. 26)

- It's common for some people to respond angrily in response to certain triggers. What triggers their anger? And what behaviors do they usually display? Is it possible to change these responses? Have students use **Awareness Window** (p. 17) or **Mood Graph** (p. 19) to discover what triggers their anger.

Let's Talk About Rules

- Talk about why we have rules in society. What society rules (laws) can they think of? What school rules can they think of? What rules do they have at home? Have rules been invented to stop people having fun? Discuss how, on the whole, we live life harmoniously because we follow rules which make our lives safer and more pleasant. If there were no school rules… what do you think it might be like here? What other rules can they think of (church, friends' houses, youth club) Use the **Rules Rule!** sheet (p. 27) to focus on these ideas.

Let's Talk About Behavior Rules

- Some of the school or class rules you know are probably related to how people are expected to behave towards each other. These rules are usually based on one idea — that we should treat others in the way we ourselves would like to be treated. Sometimes, if we get angry, we forget about this central rule. Expressions of anger commonly impinge on the rights of others. Discuss how. The sheet **Things We Should Remember When We're Angry** (p. 28) has been designed to pin up in the classroom as a memory jogger about what our 'anger rules' are. It's also appropriate for students to add to this list, or design their own rules to make into a poster.

- Talk about the kinds of things people could do when they are feeling angry that are okay. See page 35 for a list of activities for dealing with anger effectively.

Autobiography in Five Short Chapters

I.

I walk down the street.

There's a deep hole in the sidewalk.
I fall in.
I am lost.....I am helpless;

it isn't my fault.

It takes forever to find a way out.

II.

I walk down the same street.

There is a deep hole in the sidewalk.
I pretend I don't see it.
I fall in again.
I can't believe I am in the same place;

but it isn't my fault.

It still takes a long time to get out.

III.

I walk down the same street.

There is a deep hole in the sidewalk.
I see it is there.
I still fall in....it's a habit.

My eyes are open.
I know where I am.

It is my fault.
I get out immediately.

IV.

I walk down the same street.

There is a deep hole in the sidewalk.
I walk around it.

V.

I walk down another street.

Portia Nelson

Can You Break the Habit?

Think of a habit you have or a behavior you'd like to change. Look at the four personal qualities below that you need to possess if you are going to make a change. Keeping these qualities in mind, explain how you would like to go about changing your habit.

1. Self-awareness
I can stand away from myself and look at my thoughts and actions

2. Conscience
I can listen to my inner voice to know what is right and what is wrong

3. Imagination
I can see new possibilities

4. Willpower
I have the power to make choices

The habit or behavior I'd like to change is…

What I need to do to achieve this is…

Rules Rule!

Why do we have rules?

To make our lives easier?

To make our lives safer?

Think of a rule you know for each of the following

A rule of this country

What's it for?

A rule at your home

What's it for?

A rule in a sport you know

What's it for?

A rule at this school

What's it for?

A rule in this class

What's it for?

Where Does My Anger Come From? 27

Things We Should Remember When We're Angry

IT'S OKAY TO FEEL ANGRY

BUT

Don't hurt others
Don't hurt yourself
Don't hurt property
Don't plot revenge

Do take time out!
Do talk about it!

Remember

ANGER is just one letter away from **D**ANGER

2. I'm Boiling Over

Key Ideas

If people can identify their 'anger triggers' they will know better how to deal with them. How angry is 'boiling over'? What events from the past still make people angry? What do people do that might make others angry?

- Have students prepare an **Awareness Window** (p. 17) or **Mood Graph** (p. 19) to identify what makes them angry. Or, use **Knocking Down Walls** (p. 20) to help students identify and take positive steps to deal with their anger.

- As a class, compare the bricks in each student's personal space (see **Knocking Down Walls**, p. 20) to see what sources of anger they are currently trying to deal with. Or, you can review previous Awareness Windows or Mood Graphs to see what has bothered students in the past.

Feelings — Let's Talk About Different Feelings of Anger

- Discuss the levels of anger that different people feel in different situations. One person might feel rage and want to hit out when they are told off; another person might make a nasty, cutting comment. Ask – how angry do you get? Do you boil over or do you get ice cold? Look at the first activity on the **Choices** sheet (p. 31). Either use it as a discussion prompt, or fill it out.

- Look at the second activity on the **Choices** sheet. Talk about the different ways of dealing with these situations. Some students might like to role-play them with different endings.

Baggage — Let's Talk About Excess Baggage

- Everybody has had things happen in the past that can still make them feel angry in the present. The more that people hang onto old anger, the more likely they are to react angrily to similar situations in the present. Old angers and hurts can make us physically ill, so it's better to try and deal with them. What can students think of that still makes them feel angry? Share in pairs. Is there anything they can do to deal with the old anger they feel? The idea that stuff from the past can affect our present is often called "excess baggage". The more "bags" somebody carries, the harder it is for them to walk around easily. The **Excess Baggage** (p. 32) sheet provides a focus for students to look at some of this old stuff.

- Students fill in the boxes with past things they still feel angry about.

- Discuss together ways of dealing with these issues.

NOTE: particular attention to confidentiality is necessary here, "What is said in this room stays in this room." Some individual students might need follow-up assistance after this session. If in doubt, establish what you are going to do with a school counsellor or health specialist before you start.

Let's Talk About Triggering Anger in Others

- The **Angering Others** sheet (p. 33) invites students to do some self-reflection. So far they have looked at what makes *them* angry. This time they examine the things that they consciously do to make *other* people angry. The purpose is to help students understand the notion of "anger triggers" more clearly by identifying others' responses to the things they do. Ask, when was the last time someone was angry with you? What seemed to cause it? Something you did or said? Most people are aware of the things they do which can cause others to react angrily. For example, talking when the teacher does, borrowing a friend's thing without asking, leaving their bedroom untidy. If we can identify these things we can choose to change or modify our behavior so that others don't get angry with us.

- Ask students to honestly discuss the things they do that they know make people angry. Talk about whether they want to change these behaviors. Discuss strategies for change. If they don't want to change – discuss why.

Choices

Look at the choices below. Which ones best describe you when you feel angry?

When I'm angry I feel like:

A black sky

A burning line

A spike

A tornado

A volcano

A bee

A scorpion

A hammer

An iceberg

A statue

A boiling pot

A lake

Can you say why you picked these choices?
Look at other people's choices, do you agree with them?

Discuss these situations. How do you think you would react in each?

1. Your best friend accidentally sits on your lunch. You **a)** Yell at him/her **b)** laugh and say it's OK **c)** Insist that he/she goes and buys you some more lunch.

2. You are going on a bike ride with a friend. You're really excited and ready well before time. Your friend turns up late and says he/she doesn't feel like a ride now. You **a)** Say it doesn't matter and decide to do something else instead **b)** Tell your friend that you're fed up with him/her and ask for an explanation **c)** Say you didn't want to go either **d)** Shout at them, saying how unreliable they are and slam the door.

3. You've saved up for a new pair of boots. You wear them to school and a group of kids from another class laugh and tell you they look really dorky. You **a)** Swear at them and walk off **b)** Tell them they're all losers anyway and you don't care what they think **c)** Tell them you don't appreciate comments like that and walk off **d)** Kick the closest kid.

Excess Baggage

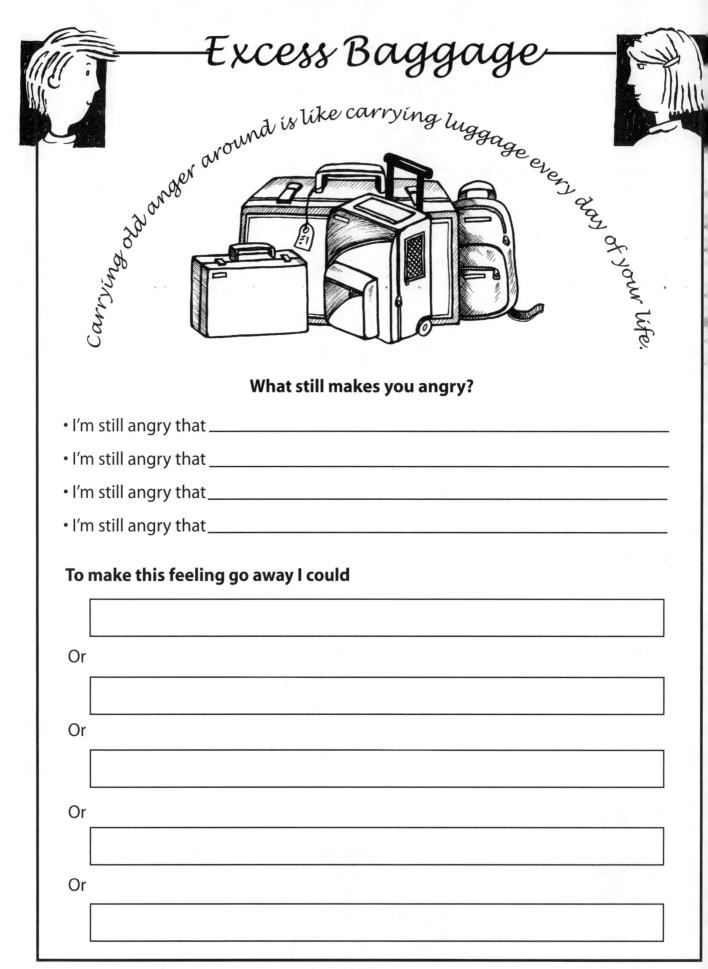

Carrying old anger around is like carrying luggage every day of your life.

What still makes you angry?

- I'm still angry that _____
- I'm still angry that _____
- I'm still angry that _____
- I'm still angry that _____

To make this feeling go away I could

Or

Or

Or

Or

Angering Others

What do you do that angers others? Come on… be honest!

• In the classroom I sometimes:

• With my classmates and friends I sometimes:

• At home I sometimes:

Some things I know I can change are:

I can do this by:

Only you have the power to change these habits!

3. Focus on the Physical

Key Ideas

When we're angry, our bodies respond in particular ways. We can learn to control these responses so that we don't hurt others or ourselves.

Starting Off Ideas

- There might be differences between individuals, but generally the physiological changes that our bodies undergo when we become angry are very similar. Ask people what happens to their bodies when they are angry. Responses might cover:

  - Nausea
  - Hands becoming fists
  - Shaking hands
  - Racing heart
  - Butterflies in stomach

  - Tense muscles
  - Speaking more loudly
  - Dry mouth
  - Holding breath
  - Red face

  - Clenching jaw
  - Sweating
  - Rapid blinking
  - Energy surges

If we learn to take note of the physical responses to anger, both our own ("OK, I can feel I'm getting angry") and other people's, ("It looks as though she's getting angry") we can learn how to control our reactions and also deal more positively with other people's anger.

Let's Talk About Physical Reactions

- Talk about body language and how signals help us to work out how others are feeling. What signals let you know that another person is bored, sad, annoyed?

- Complete the **What is Your Body Saying?** sheet (p. 44). Try to work out the actual physiological changes that people experience. Have people visualize themselves in that position. For example, if someone is anxious that they might be late for something, they might jiggle a leg. Where does the jiggling come from?

- Knowing how others are feeling by observing their body signals is useful, but it's even more useful if we can observe our own signals as they kick in. Knowing the tell-tale signs in our own bodies is the first step towards controlling our responses when we start to feel angry.

- Use the **Listen to the Legs** sheet (p. 45) to focus on individual responses. Start at the feet of the person diagram and ask students to record their own personal body signals which signal their anger around the body of the diagram. Each particular set of signals will probably be unique to each individual.

- Share responses. Look for similarities and differences.

Let's Talk About Keeping Calm

When people are angry it is harder for them to react in a positive way because they are 'thinking' with their feelings and not with their brains. To make a good decision about what to do in any situation a person needs to feel calm. The **Cool, Calm and Collected** sheet (p. 46) provides students with some ideas of ways to cool down when they are feeling angry. This provides follow-up work to the discussion on physiological reactions to anger.

- Discuss why it is necessary to calm down when we are feeling angry.
- What ideas do people have for calming their angry feelings?
- Look at the ideas on the **Cool, Calm and Collected** sheet (p. 46).

Have students try:

Counting:	Count to 10 slowly.
Speed walking:	Speed walk around the school or a designated hall. It may be appropriate to have "speed walking buddies" so an upset student is not walking alone. You may wish to practise speed walking as a class. The fast pace reduces tension and allows students to remove themselves from the place of conflict. Be sure to set a time limit for this.
Exercising:	Do jumping jacks or skip rope to clear your head.
Visualizing:	Visualize being in a place that makes you feel happy and safe. Or imagine a balloon filling up with your anger. Then imagine deflating it, slowly releasing your anger.
Writing:	Write down why you are angry.
Fist scribbling:	Hold a piece of charcoal or a thick black pencil in each fist. Then, using both fists, scribble on a large sheet of heavy paper. Students may wish to display their papers or take them home. One student was heard to say, "I want my mom to see what I did with my anger today!"
Bubble-popping:	Pop the bubbles on bubble wrap. Bubble wrap is inexpensive and can be cut into small pieces.
Blowing bubbles:	Blow bubbles. Keep a jar of bubble mixture at your desk. Students may take the bubble mixture to a spot where soap on the floor won't be a problem. Ask students to blow as many bubbles as possible within two minutes.
Pattern tracing:	Find a pattern in the room such as the carpet and trace around it with your eyes.
Breathing deeply:	Breath in through your nose and out through your mouth slowly several times.
Tube knocking:	Hit two empty paper towel tubes together to create an original rhythm or series of repeated sounds. You may ask the student to share their creation with the class.
Paper shredding:	Tearing up newspapers. Newsprint works well since it tears nicely in one direction, providing a great feeling of satisfaction.

- Consider other ways of calming down for example: having a drink, running cold water on hands. It is important that students recognize the difference between calming down and handling a situation.

- To help your class deal with anger, stress and other emotions try playing **Balloon Float** (p. 22). This game is great for students to vent their emotions in a positive and cooperative atmosphere.

Let's Talk About Words

Anger is an emotion that has a rich and colorful language to describe it. Many students have a limited vocabulary when it comes to describing the level of anger they feel which means they tend to resort to swearing to express anger. The ***Name Your Anger*** sheet (p. 47) attempts to equip students with a wider anger vocabulary and develop their awareness of the steps they can take in harnessing their anger while it is still manageable.

- Discuss degrees of anger (annoyance to fury) and how anger can escalate into something that is hard to control if initial feelings are not dealt with.

- Have students complete a **Mood Graph** (p. 19) to compare the levels of emotions they feel over the period of a day.

- Brainstorm with the students all the words that describe the feelings we have when we're angry, for example: annoyed, irritated, violent, exasperated, indignant, frustrated, furious, outraged, (whether or not swear words are permitted will be up to the discretion of the teacher but it is worth considering that within the context of the students' real life world these are likely to be legitimate forms of expression).

- Ask students to put some of these words on the thermometer ranging from "a little bit angry" to "absolutely couldn't be any madder".

- Discuss how when a person feels those degrees of anger at the bottom end of the scale they are in control but if they begin to move into those degrees of anger that describe the feelings at the top end of the scale they are in danger of losing control. To maintain control students should try to relate the degrees of anger to both the body signals each might have and the strategies they have learnt for calming themselves.

Let's Talk About Time Out

If students feel angry in class, most of them will be able to control and deal with it quickly, especially if they have been practising the strategies outlined in here. However, other students will find themselves triggered to such an intense degree that they will need to leave the classroom for a while to calm down so that their anger does not turn to physical aggression.

These students might deal with their feelings of anger by destructive behaviors like hitting and verbal abuse. In order to ensure everyone's safety, including the student involved, there needs to be a strategy in place that these students can access without a fuss. The ***Time Out Pass*** (p. 42) has been developed for these students.

The purpose of the pass is to help these students monitor and control their anger. It allows them to leave a situation of conflict (if they feel they are about to lose control) and go to a pre-specified area for a short time where they can calm down until they are able to address the situation in a positive manner. For this kind of system to work it needs to be accepted as a school-wide policy.

Suggested Time Out Procedure

- Establish who will be responsible for monitoring the time out space and where it will be located. (Ideally this should be a school-wide system but it could be established within a single classroom if necessary).

- Identify who will be eligible for a pass. It is likely that this is the small group of students who are listed on the schools special needs register as those who demonstrate aggressive behavior and are also receiving assistance from other special needs areas. This does not preclude other students using it.

- On an individual basis issue the pass to students after explaining what it is for and how to use it. Have students practise the procedure for using it then sign the pass once they are familiar with its purpose. Emphasize that it is for *emergency use* only – when all other calming down strategies aren't enough.

- Explain to all staff how the system operates and ensure substitute teachers also know about the process.

- Use the Time Out sheets following to help you establish the process.

Using "Time Out"

The purpose and procedure for time out needs to be explained to the students who need to access it. They should know that time out is for:

- calming down, away from everyone else.

- thinking about how to improve the situation.

- thinking about new ways of handling a situation, especially if the trigger for the anger is a repeat trigger.

Students also need to know that:

- time out doesn't fix things. It just keeps them and other people safe.

- there will be consequences. Taking time out means that the student and the issue or cause will be followed up. Time out must be accountable.

- when they are calmer, they must return to class and fix things.

- time out is not a punishment or a reward; it is a **strategy** for managing anger.

The Time Out Process

1. The student has permission to be a 'time out' student. This is established beforehand.

2. The student understands the time out process.

3. The student has a time out pass allocated to them which is put on the teacher's desk when he or she is afraid they might be abusive or disruptive.

4. When the teacher receives the pass, they fill out the **Time Out Log** (p. 41). The student receives the **Hassle Log** sheet (p. 13).

5. The student leaves the room without disrupting the class.

6. The student reports to a designated person who records the fact they have asked for time out.

7. The student goes to a designated time out space, stays there for an agreed amount of time and completes a reflective task. The Hassle Log is particularly useful for helping students think through the incident.

8. After the specified time the student reports back to the designated person to say that he or she is ready to return to class.

9. The student enters back into the class work without disruption.

10. After class or school the student reports to the class teacher to talk about the reflective activity and what they now need to do to fix things.

11. Teacher and student work on implementing a strategy to resolve the situation that led to the need for time out.

Ideas for the Time Out Space

These items can be left in the time out space as a way of helping students to reflect on the situation they have just left.

- Stone sack: a sack of colored stones with meaningful words written on them (e.g., compassion, tolerance) which students can hold and think about

- Paper to write on

- Doodle table: paper over a desk that students can doodle and draw on and then dispose of

- Tactile tools: koosh balls, textured materials, fur, bubble paper, cushions and so on

- Tape recorder and blank tape that students can record their angry story on

- Grudge jar: a jar which students place paper into with angry thoughts written on them and then dispose of at the end of the day.

These can also be placed in a Time Out room to create a calming atmosphere:

- Activity action: picture books, crosswords, computer game, materials to draw pictures

- Hot or cold drinks

- Soothing music

- Fish tank

Time Out Pass Holders

Name	Room	Pass Issued	Comments

Time Out Log

Name and room	Time out space	Time left	Time returned

Time Out Pass

Time out Pass

Name_____

Room_____

Time out Pass

Name_____

Room_____

Time out Pass

Name_____

Room_____

Time out Pass

Name_____

Room_____

Time Out Procedure

- **Use** time out if you think you are going to lose control of your anger.

- **Place** your pass on a teacher's desk and leave the room without disruption. The teacher will fill your time out log in.

- **Report** to _____ and collect a hassle log. They will record your visit in a book.

- **Go** to the _____ and complete the hassle log.

- **Stay** in the time out space for _____ minutes and then tell _____ you are leaving.

- **Go back** to class and give your teacher the hassle log you filled in. DO NOT disrupt anyone.

- **See** your teacher when the time seems appropriate.

- **Have some** suggestions ready for what you need to do to fix the situation.

I have read and understood the time out procedure and know how to take time out when I really need to.

Signature _____

Time Out Teacher Follow-up

Date _____ Time _____

Correct procedure followed

Hassle log completed

Teacher discussion

Conflict resolved

What is Your Body Saying?

How you can tell what people are feeling without them speaking to you. Show here the body signals that people can give when they are experiencing certain emotions.

Feeling _____

Body signal _____

Feeling _____

Body signal _____

Feeling _____

Body signal _____

Feeling _____

Body signal _____

Feeling _____

Body signal _____

Feeling _____

Body signal _____

Feeling _____

Body signal _____

Feeling _____

Body signal _____

Listen to the Legs

How do you actually feel when you get angry? What happens to your body? Use this body shape to show the physical signals you have. Use arrows and label the body parts with descriptions.

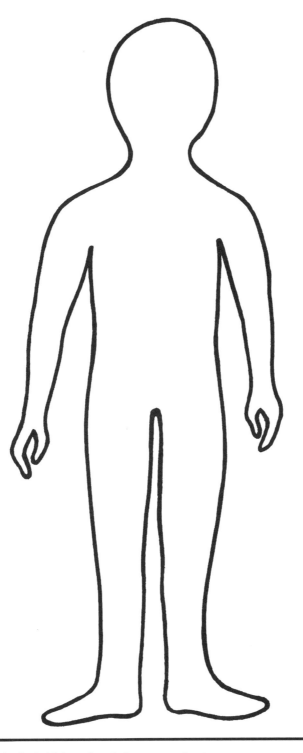

Cool, Calm and Collected

Calm yourself down by

Counting

one ... two ... three ... four ... five ... six ...

Speed walking

Exercising

Visualizing

Writing

Fist scribbling

Bubble-popping

Blowing bubbles

Pattern tracing

Breathing deeply

Tube knocking

Paper shredding

What other ideas do you have?

Name Your Anger

How many words are there for feeling angry? Do they all mean the same thing? Use the thermometer below to show the degrees of anger that it's possible to feel – and what happens at each stage. Discuss what needs to happen to help people turn down the heat. Use the **Anger Scenario** sheet to help.

Color in the thermometer.

Anger Scenarios

Look at these scenarios that can make some of us angry. Which ones would make you angry? What kind of anger would it be? Stick them on the **Name Your Anger** sheet.

There are two spaces at the bottom so that you can add your own ideas.

Being called names	Being left till last every time a team is picked
Being let down by friends	Not being allowed to watch TV
Being laughed at by the teacher	Having your chair pulled away when you go to sit on it
Being made to stay in when you want to go out	Being told off by an adult
Someone spreading rumors about you or your family	Having someone push in front of you in line
The teacher blaming you for something you didn't do	Someone borrowing your crayons/markers and then giving them to someone else
Someone borrowing your things but never bringing them back	Someone revealing a secret you told them
Being teased because you wear glasses	Having to do the dishes
Seeing someone with something you'd like – but not being able to afford it	Someone hurting an animal
Having a trick played on you	Someone doing better than you in a test
Someone being sarcastic to you	Someone not believing you when you tell them something
Being bullied by someone	Being hit by someone at home
Someone passing notes with nasty things written about you on them	Being sworn at
Someone putting your family down	People making fun of you
The teacher using put-downs to make fun of you	Someone making fun of your religion

4. Focus on Thoughts

Key Ideas

When people get angry they often **think** things that can make them feel even angrier. " I hate him!", or "She's going to get what she deserves " or "He's always picking on me! My life's not fair". Thoughts like this often lead people to handle their anger in a negative way. Consciously trying to restructure how we think when we're angry can help us address our anger more effectively.

Starting Off Ideas

Talk about what kinds of things make people in your life angry. For example friends, or brothers and sisters. What kinds of things do you say to them which might help them feel better? You probably say things like:

" It will look a lot better in the morning."
" Forget about it, he's not worth the trouble."
" This is not such a big deal, ignore it."

Statements like this help to calm others down*. You can do this for yourself too by trying to introduce more positive calming thoughts into your mind when you feel angry. It takes a bit of practice though!

*Note: These statements may help to calm others down, however, not if you are dealing with bullying. Bullying is not about resolving a conflict. Bullying is an abuse of power where one person feels unsafe and victimized. If a student experiences bullying or a student suspects bullying, they need to be encouraged to report it to a teacher.

Let's Talk About The Power of Thinking

Thinking negative thoughts influences the way we respond when we feel angry. So, can we do something about this?

- Discuss with the students how the things we say to ourselves in our heads can affect our behaviour. Draw a 1/2 glass of milk on the board. Ask people what they see — half empty or half full?

- Ask the students to think about what thoughts they have when they get mad and to write these in the lightning bolts on the ***Things I Think and Things I Could Think*** sheet (p. 53). You might need to create some 'angry making' scenarios to provide a context for this activity.

- Ask willing students to read their thoughts out loud in an angry tone and discuss the negative feelings it creates.

If a person wants to successfully eliminate 'mad' thoughts from their range of angry behaviors they have to replace those with thoughts or self-instructions and statements that make them feel calmer. Many students will only have a very limited number of self-statements that are calming, so this part of the activity will help to build students' repertoire of calming thoughts.

- Discuss with the students how saying positive things to ourselves in our heads (glad thoughts) when we are angry can help us to control our behavior.

- Ask the students to think about what thoughts they have when they get mad that are helpful in calming them down and to write these in the clouds on the ***Things I Think and Things I Could Think*** sheet (p. 53).

- Ask willing students to read their thoughts out loud in a soothing tone and discuss the feelings it creates.

- Add these possibilities to the clouds.

Let's Talk About Getting Things in Perspective

Spend some time talking about specific things that regularly make you feel angry. For example, does one of your siblings constantly do something that makes you wild? Does someone in class tease you? Identify a couple of these things and do this problem-solving exercise which focuses on getting you to think about it a different way. Use the ***Is It Worth the Fuss?*** sheet (p. 54). Ask yourself:

Is this really something worth getting angry about?
Think about it in the cool light of day. Try and pin-point exactly why you get angry. What underpins the feeling? Is it worth the effort of getting angry? Can you just 'ignore' it or 'let it go'? What would be the worst thing that could happen if you did ignore it? Do people 'bait' you so that they can enjoy seeing you get angry? What would happen if you **didn't** take the bait? Think about the last time you were angry. Did you get over it? How? It's history now, and you probably thought it was really important at the time, didn't you? It's worth keeping in mind that all things pass. Remember when you were a little kid and you got angry? You probably laugh now at the things that made you angry then.

Does anyone else get angry about the same thing?
If they do, find out how they deal with it or just talk to them to share the issue – they may be glad to talk. Talking about it may help you put it in perspective.

Can you break it down?

Think about the last time this thing made you angry. What led up to it? What happened exactly, in a step-by-step sequence? What did you say? What did the other person say? How did you feel exactly? Read through what you have written — can you identify anything there that needs to be worked on, either by you or you and the other person together to make sure you don't keep repeating the pattern?

Does it really matter anyway?

If you just let this situation go, instead of reacting to it, will it really matter anyway? If it does, will it matter in six months or a year? If it can't be fixed immediately bear in mind that you will probably have plenty of opportunities to fix it sometime. As long as you have done your best to address the anger you feel in this situation, and you try each time this situation comes up, it will improve. Remember that anger has a 'cost' — it could 'cost' you a friendship.

Let's Talk About Thinking Ahead

No matter what decision people make about how to handle a situation that has made them angry, it will have consequences. A good decision generally leads to good consequences and a poor decision will probably have bad consequences.

We can prepare ourselves to think ahead to what sorts of negative consequences the results of our anger might have. The consequences might be social (how others see and relate to us) or they might be external (we might be suspended, or stopped from doing something we like). We might end up seeing ourselves in a bad light too. Consequences can also be short (immediate) or long term (after the incident). Use the sheet ***Considering the Consequences*** (p. 55) to focus on this.

- Discuss the concept of consequences and why it is important to think about what the consequences of something might be before people act. Apply it to other things in life. What are the consequences of being late for school? Not doing homework?

- Ask students to pick one of the behaviors they choose when they are angry that is not a good choice and record it in the sentence at the top of the page under **short-term consequences** and at the bottom of the page under **long-term consequences**. Discuss the difference between short– and long–term consequences.

- Discuss and record both the short–term and long–term consequences of that choice. Repeat the process with a second example of a negative choice.

Note: Use copies of p. 55 for different kinds of consequences: social, external, how we see ourselves. Use these prompts: I feel…(Self perception) Others think…(Social) Something that could happen is…(External)

Let's Talk About Using Tools

It's not unusual to be trapped into responding in the same ways each time we find ourselves in a conflict. If we've learned to respond aggressively to conflict, we'll usually keep being aggressive until we're given some new behavior 'tools' to try.

- Talk about the idea of 'teaching an old dog new tricks' in very general terms. Do students think it's possible to change behavior? Why? Why not? Do they have any experience of changing something in their lives? How did it come about? Revisit the poem on p. 25 "Autobiography in Five Short Chapters".

- Read through the list of strategies on the **Tools of the Trade Sheet** (p. 56) and discuss the circumstances in which these might be appropriate.

- Brainstorm other positive ways to solve situations of conflict. Add these to the sheet. Use the **Anger Scenarios** on p. 48 to prompt people. "How angry would you feel in this situation? What are the ways you could respond?" Often a visual reminder or physical prompt can be a powerful tool in helping students to retain ideas. The page can be added to and laminated so that students can refer to it when they are away from a teaching and learning situation.

Things I Think and Things I Could Think

MAD THOUGHTS

GLAD THOUGHTS

Is It Worth the Fuss?

What is the situation?

Is this really something worth getting angry about?

Yes because …

No because …

Does anyone else get angry about the same thing?
How do they handle it?

Can you break it down?

Does it really matter anyway?

Why? Why not?

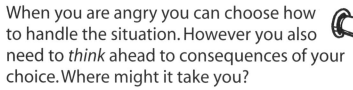 

Considering the Consequences

When you are angry you can choose how to handle the situation. However you also need to *think* ahead to consequences of your choice. Where might it take you?

Short Term Consequences

- When I am angry I could choose to

- If I do this the likely short–term consequences are

- This will mean that

- When I am angry I could also choose to

- If I do this the likely short–term consequences are

- This will mean that

Long Term Consequences

- When I am angry I could choose to

- If I do this the likely long–term consequences are

- This will mean that

- When I am angry I could also choose to

- If I do this the likely long–term consequences are

- This will mean that

Tools of the Trade

To handle anger in a way that shows you have the tools to be in control of yourself and that you feel powerful enough to make a good choice you can:

Add other ideas to this sheet!

5. Powerful Words

Key Ideas

Solving conflict in appropriate ways requires some quite advanced interpersonal skills. While we have learnt that aggression is not an appropriate way to solve problems, passivity is just as inappropriate as it can leave us feeling powerless. When we are faced with conflict, well chosen words that express our feelings and help us to state what is wrong can be the most effective strategy for reaching resolution.

Starting Off Ideas

- Discuss with the students the differences between being aggressive, passive and assertive.

- The **Say What You Mean** page (p. 60) provides students with a formula of words to use to assist them to make assertive statements in situations of conflict. Read the example of the powerful statement from the sheet then ask the students to write two examples of their own in the speech bubbles on the page. Ask students to visualize real times in their lives when they could use their powerful words. Spend some time saying them out loud.

Let's Talk About Resolving Conflict

This activity takes the powerful words 'formula' idea and applies it more broadly to resolving conflict. The idea is that, like 'knowing your words beforehand', resolving conflict can be made easier by planning a procedure of behavior to be followed too. If we have a plan for responding we are more likely to make a considered choice rather than acting on impulse.

- Talk about what conflict resolution is. For example, a conflict can be resolved by a punch on the nose, this is just not a very positive way to reach a resolution!

- Ask students to complete the stop and think section of the **Resolution Framework** (p. 61). Brainstorm current issues that could lead to conflict which students have, or make up some problems.

- Ask students to think about three possible ways to resolve the issue and record these on the sheet under the Choices heading. Students write a possible consequence for each choice under the Consequence heading.

- Ask students to pick the choice that will have the best consequence.

- Discuss the concept of evaluating the choice and selecting another option if the first choice does not work.

- Ask willing students to role-play the procedure.

Let's Talk About Negotiating

Often students find themselves feeling angry because they disagree with another person. In these circumstances knowing skills which will lead to compromise or negotiation is one way that both parties retain dignity and feel content with the outcome.

- Discuss the concept of negotiation and when it is useful to use it. Cite examples from school life (especially if you have a peer mediation programme) or the media where solutions are reached through talk. Check to see if the school already has a mediation procedure, and a teacher with experience in mediation training.

- Have students try to come up with a procedure for how this kind of negotiation can begin and proceed to its conclusion. Emphasize the need for clear guidelines. Compare the students' procedure with this commonly used procedure for resolving conflict. Look at similarities and differences.

SELF - TALK

It's important to give students opportunities to self evaluate their behavior through 'self-talk'. This strategy involves students verbally 'walking through' what happened to pinpoint exactly where things started to go wrong. It provides useful preparation for any work on resolution.

They could do this alone in a quiet space. A tape recorder might be a useful device. Students could listen to what they've said and reflect on it over time.

Talking Your Way Through Conflict

1. Someone is the facilitator. This person is impartial and manages the discussion so that both parties can tell their stories without interruption. The facilitator is in charge. Someone from another class who is not known to the people who are in disagreement would be a good choice. This person needs to be taken through the procedure carefully by a teacher first. The facilitator needs to understand how to reflect back to the parties what they are hearing to check it out, "What I think you are saying is…. Is that right?" "Joe, did you hear what Ben was saying?" The facilitator needs to understand how to use open questions. Go over the use of "I" statements.

2. The teacher should be on hand in case of problems, but should not take over. Note that this kind of conflict resolution activity is not appropriate where one person feels unsafe, for example if bullying is involved. Refer to the school's behavior management policy in this kind of circumstance.

3. Each party in the conflict is bound by the rules of the negotiation. They must agree to these rules before they begin. The rules are:

   - each person has an allotted time to tell the story of what the conflict is about

   - what is talked about remains confidential, "What's said within these walls stays within these walls."

   - to listen to the other person without interrupting them (people should write notes if they want to make a comment on what the other person is saying)

   - the facilitator helps people to tell their stories by asking questions like: What happened then? How did you feel? They are not to make comments on what is said

   - there are to be no put-downs

   - the parties are to aim to come to some kind of resolution of the conflict within the time set; if none is reached, they must agree to meet again for further negotiation.

4. Emphasize the importance of tone of voice and showing respect for the other person's opinion.

5. The process could be practised by the whole class in groups of three role playing some hypothetical disagreements.

6. Next, ask students to work in pairs on the worksheet **Now for Negotiation** (p. 62). Each section has been partially completed; they should negotiate together to complete the sections to come up with a complete negotiation process that they think would work for resolving conflicts.

7. Use the process in class on a regular basis so that students become familiar with it.

Using these words will give you the power to tell people how you feel and what you want to happen.

- **I feel** (describe how you feel)

- **When** (describe what has happened)

- **Because** (say why this makes you feel that way)

- **I would like** (what do you want to change?)

- **Or** (what will you do if it doesn't change?)

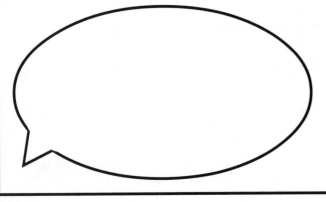

I **feel** really angry **when** you tease me **because** it does not respect my feelings and **I would like** it if you stopped saying those things **or** I will have to go and tell a teacher.

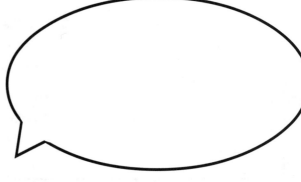

Resolution Framework

What is the problem?

How am I feeling?

How can I calm down?

What choices for resolving the conflict do you have that will have a good consequence?

Choice 1

Consequence

Choice 2

Consequence

Which is your preferred choice?

Why?

Now for Negotiation

In a calm and friendly way you can solve arguments by negotiation.

A. LISTEN WITHOUT INTERRUPTING

- Ask the other person what they consider the problem to be.
- Ask them how they are feeling.
- Say what you consider the problem to be.
- Say how you are feeling.

-
-
-
-

B. TRY TO UNDERSTAND THE ISSUES

- Take turns to ask questions.
-
-
-
-

C. RESOLVE THE ISSUES

- Say what you will do to resolve the issue.
-
-
-
-

D. ACTION AGREEMENT

- If you both agreed do what you said you would do.
-

DISAGREEMENT DECISIONS
- If you can't agree start from the beginning or get a facilitator to help you work through the process again.

---

6. Reviewing and Consolidating

Key Ideas

This last section provides a framework for reviewing and consolidating the work covered in **Keep Cool.**

Let's Talk About What We Can Remember

Like most habits, it takes a lot of effort for us to change our behavior. If we are committed to making the change and are given adequate support we will increase the likelihood of making changes, but even then we may relapse into old patterns in particularly stressful situations.

The *Learning the Lessons* pages are designed to be displayed so that students can easily remember the process they can follow to manage their feelings of anger positively.

- Talk about what's been covered so far in this work. Have students do some writing about which strategies seem most useful to them.

- Use the *Help! I Need Help!* page (p. 64) for students to draft a response to someone who is seeking advice on how to manage their anger. These can be posted on the student's personal spaces. See **Knocking Down Walls** (p. 20).

- Look over the *Learning the Lessons* pages and compare the advice with what students have in their letters.

- Decorate and display the learning the lessons page in a prominent part of the classroom as a way of reminding students what they have learnt.

- Post the students' **Awareness Windows** (p. 17) so students can see their progress.

Graduation Certificate

The graduation certificate (p. 67) serves to acknowledge the skills the students have learnt from participating in this programme and provides a way to give students public recognition that indicates the value of these skills to the school community.

Help! I Need Help!

Dear Friend

I need your help. I regularly become very angry over quite small things. It's making me unhappy because my friends are turning away from me and people at home seem to be losing patience with me. I don't know what to do. Here are the kinds of things that happen to trigger my anger:

I get angry when:
- I can't do the things I want to do
- I'm told off by anyone

Here's what I do when I get angry:
- I yell at people
- I swear and call people names
- Sometimes I hit or push people

Here's how I feel when I get angry:
- my blood seems to boil
- my heart races
- I want to lash out
- my mouth goes dry
- my jaw clenches

I don't want to be like this any more. Do you have any advice for me?

WHEN YOU'RE FEELING ANGRY REMEMBER...

that you can make a choice about how you handle your anger.

WHEN YOU'RE FEELING ANGRY REMEMBER...

to ask for Time Out if you feel overwhelmed by your feelings.

WHEN YOU'RE FEELING ANGRY REMEMBER...

that you have strategies for calming down like breathing deeply, counting, going to your happy place.

WHEN YOU'RE FEELING ANGRY REMEMBER...

that you have the tools you can use to resolve the conflict like: negotiation, talking about it, using `I' messages, walking away.

This is to certify that

_____

knows the skills for
how to Keep Cool!

Signed _____

This is to certify that

_____

knows the skills for
how to Keep Cool!

Signed _____

Reviewing and Consolidating

Index